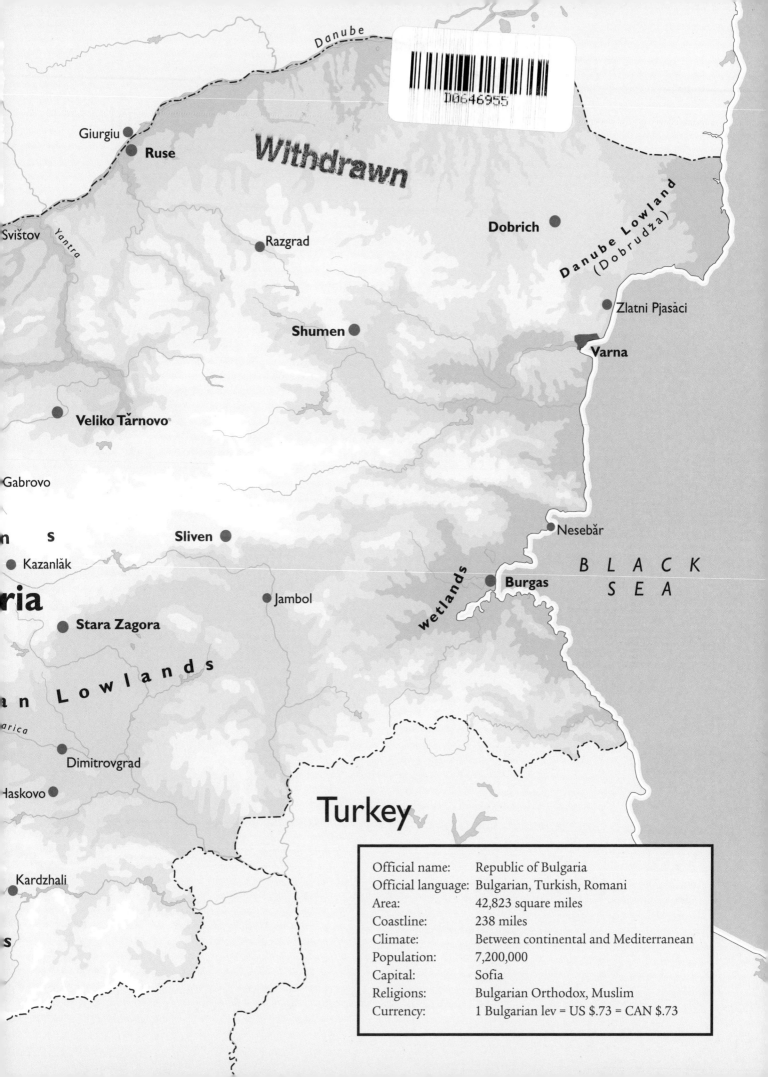

Giurgiu

Ruse

Svištov

Yantra

Razgrad

Withdrawn

Dobrich

Danube Lowland (Dobrudža)

Zlatni Pjasăci

Shumen

Varna

Veliko Tărnovo

Gabrovo

n s

Sliven

Nesebăr

Kazanlăk

Wetlands

B L A C K
S E A

ria

Jambol

Burgas

Stara Zagora

a n   L o w l a n d s

arica

Dimitrovgrad

Haskovo

Turkey

Kardzhali

s

Official name:	Republic of Bulgaria
Official language:	Bulgarian, Turkish, Romani
Area:	42,823 square miles
Coastline:	238 miles
Climate:	Between continental and Mediterranean
Population:	7,200,000
Capital:	Sofia
Religions:	Bulgarian Orthodox, Muslim
Currency:	1 Bulgarian lev = US $.73 = CAN $.73

Looking at Europe

Bulgaria

Bronja Prazdny

The Oliver Press, Inc.
Minneapolis

This edition published in 2011 by The Oliver Press, Inc.
Charlotte Square
5707 West 36th Street
Minneapolis, MN 55416-2510

Published by arrangement with KIT Publishers, The Netherlands
Copyright © 2008 KIT Publishers – Amsterdam

Library of Congress Cataloging-in-Publication Data

Prazdny, Bronja.
   [Op bezoek in Bulgarije. English]
   Bulgaria / Bronja Prazdny.
         p. cm. -- (Looking at Europe)
   Includes index.
   ISBN 978-1-881508-85-4
   1. Bulgaria--Juvenile literature. I. Title.
   DR67.7.P73 2010
   949.9--dc22

                                                    2009032670

Text: Bronja Prazdny
Photographs: Bronja Prazdny p. 3, 5 (t), 7 (m), 8 (b), 15 (m), 17 (t/m), 20 (t/m), 22 (t/b),
23 (t/ml/b), 25, 26 (t), 27 (tr), 28 (t/m), 32, 33 (t) 34 (t), 39 (m), 40 (t); Nenko Lazarov p. 7 (b), 29
(b), 36 (b), 37 (b), 46 (t); Tanya Gin Barton p. 10 (t), 12 (t/b), 21 (m/b), 22 (m), 30 (t), 31, 34 (b),
35 (b), 38 (b), 42 (t), 47 (m); Per Palmkvist p. 16 (t), 28 (b), 33 (b); Ivan S. Abrams p. 18 (t/m),
29 (t), 35 (m), 37 (m), 38 (b), 45 (m); Sarah Ramspott p. 24 (b); Marjan van Hoogenbemt p. 40
(b); Todor Trundrev p. 42 (b); Kiril Kapustin p. 45 (b) and 46 (m/b); Ries van Wendel de Joode.
www.imagesfrombulgaria.com: Peter Iankov p. 47 (b); Pascal Reusch p. 47 (t).

Translation: Louisa Spenceley
US editing: Anna Aman
Design and Layout: Miranda Zonneveld, Alkmaar, The Netherlands
Cover: Icon Productions, Minneapolis, USA
Cartography: Armand Haye, Amsterdam, The Netherlands
ISBN 978-1-881508-85-4
Printed in The United States of America
14 13 12 11   5 4 3 2 1

Contents

Pronunciation of Bulgarian
ă = u (as in pudding)
c = tz / ts (as in tsar)
č = ch (as in choice)
ch = k (as in skate)
š = sh (as in short)
u = ou (as in group)
ž = g (as in gentle)

Introduction

Bulgaria lies on the Balkan Peninsula in the southeast of Europe. It is surrounded by Greece, Macedonia, Serbia, Romania, and Turkey. The Black Sea lies to the east of Bulgaria. The people speak Bulgarian, which is a South Slavic language. Bulgarians use the Cyrillic alphabet. Pronunciations of Bulgarian letters can be found on the previous page.

Various peoples ruled Bulgaria before the First Bulgarian Empire was established in 681. The Turks of the Ottoman Empire ruled Bulgaria for nearly five centuries, from the end of the fourteenth century until 1878. Bulgaria then became a self-governing state. After World War II, Bulgaria became part of the Eastern Bloc, the group of Eastern European countries under communist control. In 1989, after the fall of communism, Bulgaria became a parliamentary democracy. Bulgaria joined the European Union on January 1, 2007.

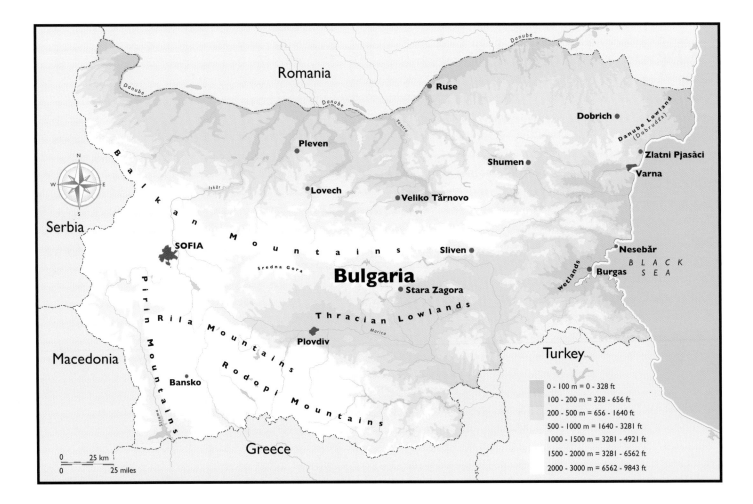

History

At the beginning of the seventh century, the territory that is now Bulgaria was populated by two peoples: the Slavs and the Proto-Bulgarians. Together, they founded the First Bulgarian Empire in 681. Bulgarians today are descendants of these two peoples.

The Thracians

Thracians lived in Bulgaria before the arrival of the Slavs and the later arrival of the Proto-Bulgarians. Exactly where the Thracians came from and what language they spoke is unknown. They no longer exist and their language was never written down. However, archaeologists have been able to excavate places where this ancient civilization flourished. Recently, a golden mask, rings, and other objects were found that had belonged to a Thracian king.

▲ *Roman gate and walls in the town of Hisar (also known as Hissarya)*

Even before the Thracians, Bulgaria was ruled by other empires. In the first century BC, the Thracians were brought under the control of the Romans. Later, the territory became part of the Byzantine Empire.

The First and Second Bulgarian Empire (681–1396)

The Slavs moved into the Balkans in the sixth century and settled in the east of the country. The Slavic and Thracian peoples intermarried and, over time, Thracian culture was overtaken by the Slavic culture.

A century later, the Proto-Bulgarians invaded the country. They were a Turco-Mongolian nomad people from Central Asia. The two tribes, the Slavs and the Proto-Bulgarians, then intermarried and became the Bulgarians. Together they defeated the Byzantines under the leadership of Asparuhk Khan and founded the First Bulgarian Empire. The Empire expanded and in the ninth and tenth centuries covered large parts of the former Yugoslavia, Albania, the north of Greece, and the whole of Romania. During this time, the Empire was ruled by tsars. Bulgaria was proclaimed a Christian country in 865 during the reign of Tsar Boris I.

▶ *Rila Monastery was built during the reign of Peter I in the tenth century. He was the successor of Tsar Simeon I.*

The First Bulgarian Empire lasted until 1018. Then it again came under the control of the Byzantine Empire. The Bulgarians fought to rid themselves of this foreign control and finally succeeded in 1185. That year, two Bulgarian *bojars* (noble landowners), Petăr and Asen, led a successful revolt against the Byzantines. This was the beginning of the Second Bulgarian Empire. Veliko Tărnovo became the new capital city. Petăr and Asen's youngest brother, Tsar Kalojan, also succeeded in regaining some land from the Byzantines. However, Bulgaria never became as large as it once was. The surrounding countries had become too strong.

At first, the economy flourished, as did trade and Bulgarian culture. Due to fighting among the *bojars*, however, the empire went into decline. A weakened Bulgaria was no match for the advancing Ottoman Turks. In 1393, the Turks occupied the Bulgarian capital, Veliko Tărnovo. A couple of years later, the Ottoman Empire conquered the whole of Bulgaria. Their rule lasted for nearly five centuries.

Five centuries of Turkish Rule (1396–1878)

Life for the Bulgarians was hard during the rule of the Turkish sultans. It was difficult for people to survive because they were forced to pay extremely high taxes. They suffered under the cruelty and corruption of local and provincial officials. Even some of the clergy abused their power. The sultan had abolished the Bulgarian patriarchy (spiritual leader of the church). He then put all Orthodox (Byzantine) churches under the rule of the Patriarchate, the spiritual leader of Constantinople. This concentration of power in Constantinople produced many corrupt clergy. Though Islam had not been officially proclaimed as the state religion, one had to be Muslim in order to occupy a high-ranking position. This is the reason why many Bulgarian nobles converted to Islam. The ordinary people remained loyal to the Bulgarian Orthodox Church, although this was not always easy. During five centuries little changed for them. Many of the changes happening elsewhere in Europe passed by Bulgaria.

◀ The Banja Baši Mosque (1576) in Sofia is one of the oldest mosques in Europe. It is also the only one in use in Sofia. Banja Baši means "washing a lot."

We are all waiting for the same bus...

In the nineteenth century, Sultan Abdul Mejid I developed and expanded commercial and cultural ties with Western countries. The sultan wanted to transform the Ottoman Empire into a modern (Western) state. He also wanted to end religious discrimination. For the Bulgarians, this was a sign that they should demand their own church, free from the Patriarchate of Constantinople. However, the Patriarchate fiercely resisted this demand. It was not until 1870 that the sultan declared the independence of the Bulgarian Church.

In the Slavejkov Square

Eva is catching her breath on a bitterly cold November day in the town center of Sofia. She looks for a place to sit. "There's more than enough room beside these two gentlemen," says Eva. She sits on the bench beside the statues of Petko Slavejkov and his son, Penčo. The square is named after these two nineteenth-century poets. In addition to poetry, the elder Petko wrote many revolutionary articles. He was committed to winning Bulgarian freedom from the Ottomans.

▲ *The ceiling of the fifteenth century Trojan Monastery in the Stara Planina Mountains. Vasil Levski enjoyed coming here.*

Vasil Levski, a national hero

Vasil was born in 1837 in the town of Karlovo, then part of the Ottoman Empire. His real name was Vasil Ivanov Kuncěv. Levski means "lion-like." He got his nickname because of a great jump he made during a military exercise. According to his friends, he also looked remarkably like a lion. Levski was dedicated to making Bulgaria a free country. A network of revolutionary groups was set up under Levski's leadership. The groups stayed in contact with each other and carried out violent campaigns against the Ottoman officials. In 1872, Levski was arrested. He was executed a couple of months later in Sofia. However, the revolutionary groups persisted. They organized the April Revolt of 1876, which failed. It did, however, help to spark the Russo-Turkish War that eventually led to a free and independent Bulgaria.

Striving for independence

By the 1870s, cultural nationalism began to grow in Bulgaria. Bulgarian nationalists wrote accounts of past glory. Battles fought long ago were praised and often made bigger and more impressive than they really were. Bulgarian heroes from the past were brought forward and honored. Bulgaria's own language and religion were also honored. Besides the call for more Bulgarian culture, there was also a desire to break away from the Ottomans. Bulgarians organized themselves into revolutionary groups.

One of the pioneers of this freedom movement was Vasil Levski. This cost him his life, as the Ottoman authorities hanged him in 1873.

◀ *Vasil Levski*

The April Revolt of 1876

Radical nationalists demanding political independence wanted to eliminate Turkish rule. If necessary, they would resort to violence. The Turks reacted by using extreme violence themselves; they could tolerate cultural and religious freedom, but they could not tolerate violence that was meant to destroy their authority. The fighting cost thousands of people their lives, including many children. Western European countries were outraged at the amount of blood being spilled. Partly for economic reasons, Western leaders did not interfere in the conflict. To the east, however, Russia wanted to gain more political and military influence in Bulgaria and now saw its chance. Russia declared war on the Ottoman sultan. Shocked by the violent response of the Turks, the Western powers did not stand in Russia's way.

San Stefano and Berlin (1878)

When the fighting ended, Russia had defeated Turkey. In the Treaty of San Stefano in March 1878, the Turks agreed to establish an independent Great Bulgaria. Great Bulgaria would stretch from the Danube River in the north to the Aegean Sea in the south. Western powers, however, were alarmed by the creation of an enormous Bulgarian state that was friendly to Russia. They forced the Russians to sign the Treaty of Berlin, which revised the earlier treaty and gave Macedonia back to the Ottomans. The Bulgarians were furious, viewing the loss of Macedonia as a national disaster. In 1887, Ferdinand of Saxe-Coburg-Gotha, a German prince, ascended the Bulgarian throne. In 1908, he declared Bulgaria an independent nation and named himself tsar.

▲ The Treaty of San Stefano was signed here.
▼ View of Melnik. The village is in the Bulgarian part of the Macedonian region, which extends over several countries.

The Macedonian question

Macedonia is a Balkan state west of Bulgaria. In the past, it formed part of southern Bulgaria. Other parts belonged to Serbia and Greece. These countries all have historical claims to Macedonia, which has been called the powder keg of the Balkans. From about 1850 to 1945, wars were fought over the question "To whom does this region actually belong?" For the Bulgarians, Macedonia is still a sore spot. A lot of people think that Macedonians are actually Bulgarians and that Macedonian is a Bulgarian dialect, a form of the Bulgarian language. Officially, however, there is no "Macedonian minority" in Bulgaria.

▶ *Bulgarian soldiers position themselves for battle.*

The Balkan Wars (1912-1913)

The Bulgarians could not accept the loss of Macedonia. Their neighbors, the Serbs and the Greeks, also thought Macedonia belonged to them. In 1912, the countries jointly decided to drive the Turks out and divide Macedonia among themselves. In just two months, the Turks lost nearly all of their European possessions to these three countries. But then Macedonia had to be divided. This was a problem because nobody wanted to give up the newly conquered territory. In June of 1913, Bulgaria declared war on its former ally, Serbia. In response, Romania, Greece, and Turkey all attacked Bulgaria. The Second Balkan War cost the Bulgarians much of the land they had previously conquered, including losing South Dobrudža to Romania and a large part of Macedonia to Serbia.

World War I (1915–1918)

During World War I, Bulgaria joined Germany and Austria, attempting to regain the territories previously lost in the Balkan Wars. With the defeat of Germany and its allies in 1918, Bulgaria lost its access to the Aegean Sea and was forced to pay reparations to the victorious countries. Reparations were payments to restore the treasuries of the countries Bulgaria had gone to war against. The enormous Bulgarian army also had to be demobilized, or made inactive.

The inter-war period (1919–1940)

The first post-war government was led by Aleksandăr Stambolijski, the Agrarian Party leader. It introduced farming reforms and tried to combat hunger and poverty. However, in 1923, opponents brought his government down and Stambolijski was murdered. His successor, Alexander Tsankov, was a violent anti-communist. Under his leadership, many communists and Agarian Party supporters were arrested or executed. In 1934, the military carried out a *coup*, a violent overthrow of the government, which reduced Tsar Boris III to the status of a puppet king. The new authoritarian government banned trade unions and political parties. A year later, Boris III staged a counter-coup that essentially made him a dictator.

◀ *Memorial for Boris III and his wife, presented by the Jewish community. During World War II, Boris worked to protect Bulgarian Jews from the Nazis, who wanted to deport them to the death camps.*

◀ *Monument in Ruse, which reads "Eternal glory for the heroes who died in the battle against Fascism"*

World War II (1941–1944)

During the 1930s, Boris III was greatly impressed with the success Adolf Hitler had in rebuilding Germany. Hitler, seeing an ally in Boris, forced the Romanians to return the region of South Dobrudža to Bulgaria in 1940. In March 1941, Bulgaria joined Nazi Germany and Fascist Italy. The Germans were allowed to cross Bulgarian territory to attack Greece. After this, the Western powers declared war on Bulgaria.

Though allied with Germany, Boris refused to help attack Russia. Nor did he allow Jews to be deported from Bulgaria, much to Hitler's displeasure. In August 1943, Boris died under mysterious circumstances, with many people suspecting that Hitler was behind his death. Simeon II, only five years old, succeeded his father, but because he was too young to rule alone, a regency was appointed. Meanwhile, more and more acts of resistance were carried out against the Germans and the Bulgarian regime. The Partisans, members of the armed resistance, worked closely with the Russians. They formed an organization called the Fatherland Front.

When it became clear that Germany would lose the war, the Bulgarian government immediately started to negotiate with the Allies. In August 1944, a pro-Western government in Bulgaria quickly declared war on Germany. But it was already too late. On the night of September 8 to 9, 1944, Russian tanks rolled into Bulgaria. The communists would soon take power.

Communist Bulgaria (1944–1989)

In 1944, the Fatherland Front staged a coup and seized control of the government. Although there were Bulgarians in the new government, the Russians were really the ones in power. The communists dealt harshly with people who had worked with the Germans. The three regents who had governed in young Simeon's name, including his uncle Kiril, were killed. Simeon was forced to flee from the country and eventually settled in Spain. A tribunal condemned thousands of people to death after they had been branded as collaborators, or traitors.

After the elimination of the monarchy in 1946, a People's Republic was proclaimed. The head of state, or premier, was Georgi Dimitrov, who was also the first secretary of the Communist Party. All other political parties were forbidden. It became obvious that Bulgaria was under the rule of the Russians, especially when a new Russian-like constitution was adopted in 1947.

▼ *Josef Stalin (left) and Georgi Dimitrov in 1936 in Moscow*

▶ *A 1969 Soviet stamp in honor of the 25-year-old Socialist Revolution in Bulgaria. It reads: "The friendship between the USSR (Soviet Union) and the Bulgarian people—indestructible for eternity."*

Stalinism

A five-year period of ruthless Stalinist rule followed the death of Dimitrov in 1949. The Bulgarian Communist Party (BCP) loyally followed the Soviet Union, where Josef Stalin ruled. Bulgaria was closed off from the outside world, having contact with just the Soviet Union and other communist countries. Agriculture was made collective, with private farms taken from their owners by the state and laborers forced to work on them. Industry was nationalized, meaning that companies and factories now belonged to the government. This controlled economy brought a higher standard of living to some, but it also limited freedom for everyone. Work camps were set up in which "enemies of the state" were imprisoned. Opponents of communism were tried in "show trials," where they were not allowed to defend themselves. The Bulgarian Orthodox Church was placed under state control. The Turkish minority was persecuted. Border disputes with Yugoslavia and Greece about Macedonia arose again.

> When Stalin, the leader of the Soviet Union, died, his brutal rule came to an end. From 1953 onwards, life in Bulgaria became less harsh, but hardly pleasant, even as work camps were closed and show trials stopped.

The Živkov Period

From 1954 to the fall of communism in 1989, the leader of Bulgaria was Todor Živkov. Slowly but surely, he drew all power into his own hands. He helped family and friends gain positions of power in the country. Živkov started out as a leader of the BCP and in 1962 became premier. In 1971, he also became president. Živkov strengthened relationships with the West, but this did not mean that he gave his people more freedom. The aim of his regime was actually to cut off the freedom of the people. There was no freedom of speech, the press, or religion.

▼ *The mosque in the village of Černo Očene in the south of Bulgaria. In this area, the population is mainly Turkish.*

"Bulgarianization" of the Turks and other Muslims

The attempt by Todor Živkov's communist government to assimilate the Bulgarian Turks and other Muslims is not a proud moment in Bulgarian history. Between 1984 and 1989, these minorities were forced to assume Slavic or Christian names and give up wearing distinctive clothing. Mosques were closed and speaking Turkish on the street was prohibited. Protests against this loss of freedom were met with violence. In 1989, more than 300,000 Muslims fled the country. After the fall of communism, the rights of the Turkish and Muslim minority were restored and many returned to Bulgaria. Although the unfair laws have been struck down, the Turks are still discriminated against in daily life, especially economically. Many of Bulgaria's Muslims, who make up about 12 percent of the country's population, believe that they are often seen as second-class citizens. They hope that with Bulgaria's entry into the European Union this perception will begin to change.

Under Živkov, Bulgaria prospered economically. But in the 1980s, the situation changed. The economy declined and Živkov was unable to do anything to improve it. More and more people expressed their dissatisfaction with Živkov's leadership. They demanded the same kind of economic reforms that had been introduced in the Soviet Union under party leader Mikhail Gorbachev. Živkov had great difficulty silencing his opponents. Nonetheless, his rigid, corrupt government heavily resisted the new Russian dogma. While the Soviets attempted to promote *glasnost* (openness) and *perestroika* (reforms) in order to improve economic and political conditions, the Bulgarian party leaders kept to their old ways. They pronounced that all the Russian "novelties" were evil. The changes, however, could not be stopped. On November 10, 1989, Todor Živkov resigned under pressure from the BCP. He had held power for 35 years.

A difficult road to democracy

The transition from communism to democracy was bumpy. The two major political parties, the Socialists (previously the Communists) and the anti-communists, fought for the majority in the government. Leadership roles for each party changed often until 1997. In the meantime, life for the ordinary Bulgarian was difficult. A few people with connections to corrupt politicians became wealthy once state control of the economy ended.

Real economic reforms only started when the economist Ivan Kostov became prime minister in 1997. Kostov introduced free-market measures to boost economic growth. The majority of state enterprises were privatized, or returned to private ownership, and Kostov tried to put the communist past behind him. The old communists were removed from important positions. However, Kostov did not know what to do with the growing corruption among government officials. The Bulgarians lost confidence in him. In 2001, Kostov was succeeded by King Simeon II (Sakskoburggotski), who had been banished as a child.

Simeon II continued Kostov's reforms. In 2004, Bulgaria joined NATO and, together with Romania in 2007, Bulgaria became a member of the European Union. Since 2006, Bulgaria has had a coalition government in which several parties work together.

◄ *The National Palace of Culture in Sofia, home for many cultural events*

Country

Bulgaria, officially Republika Bǎlgarija, lies on the Balkan Peninsula and borders five neighboring countries and the sea.

▲ *Belintaš Plateau in the Rodopi Mountains*

To the north there is Romania (380 miles of border, of which 293 miles are along the Danube River). In the south, Bulgaria borders Turkey and Greece. To the west lies Macedonia and Serbia. The Black Sea forms the 238 miles of the eastern border.

With an area of 42,823 square miles, Bulgaria is about the size of the state of Tennessee. At the end of 2010, it had about 7.2 million inhabitants. There are large parts of the country that are barely populated and some that are unpopulated. The population density is around 168 people per square mile. Of the total population, 72 percent live in cities and towns. Fifty years ago, two thirds of the population lived in the country.

The landscape

The landscape in Bulgaria is varied. It resembles Austria with its mountains, Alpine meadows with wild flowers, and fertile valleys. There are three different geographic zones: the Danube Lowland in the north, the Balkan mountains in the center running east to west, and the mountains of Rila, Pirin, and Rodopi to the southwest and south.

The Danube Lowland

The Danube Lowland, also called the Danube Bulgaria, is in the north. It is low-lying, with many hills and forests. It is about 630 feet above sea level. Forested hills alternate with wide open grassy plains (similar to a steppe, which is treeless and level). At harvest time, you can see mile upon mile of yellow fields because wheat, barley, mustard seed, and sunflowers are grown here. It is a very fertile region. The northeastern part is called Dobrudža. It is also known as the "Granny of Bulgaria."

▼ *Mustard plants in Dobrudža*

◄ *The Rajsko Praskalo waterfall just below the summit of Mount Botev, the highest peak of the Balkan Mountains*

The Stara Planina, also known as the Balkan Range, lies to the south. This massive mountain range runs right through the country from east to west. It stretches from the Black Sea in the east to Sofia, where it turns northwest. It crosses the Serbian-Bulgarian-Romanian border and then goes over into the Carpathians. The Sredna Gora Mountain Range lies just south of the Stara Planina. The extensive Balkan Range, about 375 miles long, forms a natural barrier. It divides Bulgaria in half. This mountain range consists of three regions: The High Balkan (in the north) and the West and East Balkan. The highest peak in the High Balkan by far is Botev (7,841 feet).

The Thracian Lowlands lie south of the Balkan Mountains. It is hilly there, with fertile plains on which much agricultural produce is grown.

Another mountain range lies in the southwest of the country. It is made up of three massifs (geological formations): in the north, the Rila and the Pirin Mountains, and in the south, the Rodopi Massif, which goes far into Greece. The highest Bulgarian peak is the Musala in the Rila Range (9,625 feet). Musala comes from the Turkish *Moes-Allah*, meaning "Allah's Mountain." It was given its name by the Ottoman rulers.

Above the tree line, high in the mountains, you will find only bare rocks and a few small mountain lakes. However, the lower lying mountains, especially the Rodopi Massif, are very green. Here you will find rough forests and Alpine meadows covered with unusual flowers, such as the rare and protected edelweiss. This is where Bulgarians like to go hiking and enjoy nature.

▶ *The Rajsko Praskalo ("heavenly mist") in winter*

Vitoša

South of the capital Sofia lies Mount Vitoša (6,045 feet). You can see it from the city. Even though it is nothing more than a big dome-shaped piece of stone and certainly is not one of Bulgaria's loveliest mountains, it is still worth climbing. It is not just good exercise, but also an escape from the pollution in the capital. The northern mountainside is wooded. Vitoša was created during a volcanic eruption.

▲ Stream in the Rila Mountains
▼ The Ribnoto Ezero, "Lake of Fish," is one of the Seven Rila Lakes.

The coastal plain in the east is the lowest part of the country. The northern part of the plain, with the town of Varna at its focal point, is rugged and rocky with red colored cliffs. To the south there are many small rocky bays with Mediterranean vegetation. Burgas is the biggest town there.

One-third of Bulgaria consists of high mountain ranges. Another one-third of the country has been built upon. The remaining one-third is grassland and low mountains with vineyards and large market gardens.

Rivers and lakes

Bulgaria has 526 rivers! All the rivers north of the Balkan Mountains flow into the Danube, and then into the Black Sea. All rivers south of these mountains flow into the Aegean Sea. A few small rivers in the east of the country flow directly into the Black Sea. Only the Danube, the border river with Romania, is navigable. This means it is wide enough and deep enough for boats and ships. After the Volga River, the Danube is the longest river in Europe. The Iskǎr is the longest river in Bulgaria (230 miles). It begins in Lake Čamovsko at 8,250 feet in the Rila Mountains. From there it flows through eastern Sofia and through a valley in the Balkan Mountains further northward into the Danube.

Glacial lakes

Glacial lakes were formed from melting glaciers at the end of the Ice Age. Bulgaria has nearly 200, especially high in the Rila and Pirin Mountains. In the Rila Range there are about 150 ice lakes between the high peaks. The highest lies at 8,910 feet. The Seven Rila Lakes are the most beautiful and also the most visited. The highest of these seven is Sǎlzata Ezero, known as the "Lake of Tears" (120 feet deep). Its waters are so clear that you can see right down to the bottom. Another lake is called Okoto, which means "the eye." It was given this name because it is almost perfectly oval.

◀ *Mother and son in early spring. In recent years, it seems as if winter skips spring and goes straight to summer.*

Climate

The climate in Bulgaria varies by region. In the north, the climate is continental, similar to central Europe, with very cold winters and hot summers. The Balkan Mountains and the Black Sea greatly influence this weather. South of the Balkan Mountains the weather is gentler because these mountains form a natural barrier against harsher weather. The closer one gets to Greece, the more Mediterranean the climate becomes. In the summer the temperature can rise significantly, especially on the coast. Fortunately, the sea breeze does moderate the heat. The annual rainfall is 2–2.75 inches. In the mountains, the average is almost 4 inches of rainfall. The roads through the mountain passes are often filled with snow and closed to all traffic.

National symbols

• The Bulgarian flag has three horizontal stripes: white, green, and red. The white stands for peace, the green for nature, and the red for the blood shed over the centuries and the deaths of Bulgarian warriors.

• The Bulgarian national anthem is called *Mila Rodino*, "Beloved (or precious) fatherland." In 1964, this became the official anthem. Often the text was forcibly changed. The last time was in 1990, when the communist era came to an end.

• The unit of money that Bulgarians use is called the *lev*. There are 100 *stotinki* in one lev. One hundred *leva* are worth about 70 U.S. dollars. There are a lot of counterfeit, or fake, bank notes in circulation. The 20-lev bill is the one that is faked the most. If a bill's watermark is the lion, a Bulgarian national symbol, then it is a real one.

The Balkans: mountains and region

The name "Balkan" refers to both the peninsula in the southeast of Europe as well as the mountain range that runs through Bulgaria. For many years, the name has been associated with political unrest. Wars in the region have been called the "Balkan Wars." People who live in the region prefer the term Southeast Europe. The region consists of Bulgaria, Greece, Serbia, Macedonia, Bosnia-Herzegovina, Kosovo, Montenegro, and Albania. These are countries whose territories were ruled for centuries by the Ottoman Turks. Some people think that Croatia, Slovenia, Romania, and the European part of Turkey are also part of the Balkans.

• The Bulgarians consider the Balkan Mountains to be the true symbol of their country. They call them the *Stara Planina*, meaning "Old Mountain." *Balkan* is Turkish for "forested mountain." Bulgarians only use the name "Balkan" to refer to the peninsula. They glorify their mountains in poems, stories, and songs. It is the first thing they mention in their national anthem.

◀ *A bill with the portrait of Dr. Peter Beron (1799-1871), scientist, language modernizer, and founder of modern Bulgarian grammar*

Cities

Over the course of very few years, millions of people moved from the Bulgarian countryside to the towns, where they could find work.

In 1900, only 20 percent of all Bulgarians lived in towns. Now, this number has been reversed. Nearly 72 percent live in towns and the remainder live in the countryside. The capital, Sofia, has the most inhabitants, more than 1.2 million.

Sofia

The number of people living in Sofia has increased dramatically since the end of the nineteenth century. In 1887, the city only had 21,000 inhabitants. Thirteen years later there were 47,000 and in 1946 more than 500,000 people lived there! By 2011, this number had more than doubled. The population density in the capital is about 1,600 people per square mile. This is not very much compared to a city like London, with a population density of 12,331 people per square mile.

Sofia lies in the western part of the country at the foot of Mount Vitoša. During the weekend, Mount Vitoša is busy. The people of Sofia like to hike up their favorite mountain. The city is the seat of government and of parliament. It is also where the president lives. A lot of international companies have their headquarters in Sofia and the stock exchange is based there. Sofia is also a university city. It has seventeen universities and colleges.

The city has good public transportation, with a subway, buses, trams, and trolleybuses. You have to buy your ticket (*bilet* in Bulgarian) at a station and stamp it yourself using the machine in the tram or bus. A ticket costs about fifty cents.

▲ *Apartments in Sofia*

▲ *Book stalls in Slavejkov Square*

◀ *Count Ignatiev Street in the center of Sofia*

Even though Sofia has popular restaurants, bars, and fancy dress shops, it still has an atmosphere that is totally different from Amsterdam, Brussels, or London. The buildings look different. They are often dirty and run-down. This is due to both the use of brown coal for heating and car exhaust fumes. The majority of people don't have much money. And there are a lot of beggars, often young children or disabled elderly people. There are also a lot of stray dogs in the streets. They can be dangerous though, so don't pet them!

Playing chess in a Sofia park

Bulgarians playing chess in the park is a common sight, and indeed a national passion. Bulgarians often comment on the way their friends play chess. Ivan: "I am retired and come here at least five times a week, except when it rains. Here, I meet all my friends. It is really fun. Sometimes we play for money, but most of the time we play friendly games just for fun." The game is so popular that many Bulgarians view chess masters as national heroes.

Now if I just use my knight to capture his pawn...

Sofia is one of the oldest cities in Europe. It was founded by the Thracian tribe of the Serdi in 800 BC. It was known as Serdica. The city was conquered at least five times during its long history and changed its name more than once. You can find out a lot of information on the history of Sofia in the collection at the National Museum of Archaeology. The museum has more than 650,000 artifacts from the time of the Thracians, the Romans, and the Greeks. The city's buildings display a variety of styles from different historical periods. The oldest building is Saint Gregory's Church, built by the Romans in the fourth century. It's located between the Sheraton Hotel and the remains of old Serdica. The early medieval frescos (wall paintings) are well preserved and worth seeing. During the Ottoman Empire, the church was used as a mosque and a thick coat of paint covered the frescos. They were only rediscovered in the last century.

◄ *The Alexandăr Nevsky Cathedral with its golden dome. Artisans worked on this cathedral for thirty years.*

When Sofia became the capital in 1879, the king at that time ordered the construction of many new buildings. One of them was the Alexandăr Nevsky Cathedral. It was built in 1912 in memory of Russian soldiers who died during the Russo-Turkish War (1877-1878). There are many buildings in Sofia from the communist era. These buildings are typically large, bleak, concrete tower blocks that are very ugly. Sofia, however, has more than just art, culture, history, and architecture. There are also many places to have fun, such as the Sofia Zoo. Founded in 1888, it is the oldest zoo in Bulgaria.

Walk along the Vitoša Boulevard

Known locally as the *Vitoška*, the boulevard is lined with boutiques and shops full of expensive designer clothes. It is one of the most expensive shopping streets in the world, even by Western standards. Just strolling around and looking at the people shopping for these items can be as much fun as looking at the items themselves. Stepping onto this street is like entering a whole other world. Women with dyed blond hair and men wearing gold jewelry and expensive, specially made suits walk up and down the boulevard with their sunglasses on. Walking between the Armani and Vuitton shops, you almost forget that most people earn around 250 dollars a month. Only the many beggars wrapped in rags remind you that you are in a poor country.

Plovdiv

Plovdiv is 94 miles southeast of Sofia. It has 342,000 inhabitants and is the second largest city in the country. Plovdiv lies at the foot of the Rodopi Mountains, nestled between six hills in the fertile Thracian Lowlands. Fruits and vegetables are grown in the Plovdiv province and often taken to the many food processing plants in the area. The river Marica flows right through Plovdiv; six bridges connect the two sides of the town. Plovdiv, just like Sofia, was originally a Thracian town that belonged to a number of empires. Archaeological remains have been found dating as far back as the end of the seventh century BC. Many Roman and Byzantine cultural treasures have been preserved. These include an entire large Roman amphitheater from the second century.

◀ *The amphitheater of Plovdiv. During the summer there are theatrical performances here.*

Just the two of us ...

In love in Plovdiv
This young couple is enjoying a lovely day—and each other. They look over the city that lies at their feet. The view from the side of this mountain, one of six in Plovdiv, is breathtaking. Since the couple has decided to sit up so high, they probably won't encounter too many other people on the mountain.

After Sofia, Plovdiv is the most important cultural and tourist center of Bulgaria. The old town center is very special. It is one of the most beautiful places in Bulgaria. Its small cobblestone streets lead you up to a very steep slope. Both sides of the street are lined with beautiful houses in "Bulgarian renaissance" style from the nineteenth century. They bear the names of the rich merchants and noblemen who once occupied them. Many of the houses are now used as museums or restaurants.

▼ *A little street in Plovdiv*

The Port of Varna

Varna is known as the Pearl of the Black Sea. It is the third largest city in Bulgaria and has 325,000 inhabitants. Varna also has a large harbor. The city and especially its beaches are popular tourist destinations. Millions of visitors, most of them foreigners, visit Varna every year. About 12.5 miles north of Varna is the resort area of Zlatni Pjasăci, or Golden Sands. This town has a 3.5-mile-long beach with many hotels, restaurants, cafés, and a boulevard. Although Zlatni Pjasăci is lovely, the area is often crowded and has become expensive to visit.

In Varna itself you can see art treasures from various periods. The Roman thermal baths from the third century are very unusual. Parts of these gigantic excavations can be seen in the city between the streets and houses, while some ancient ruins are still buried under ground.

▶ *The Cathedral of Varna dates from 1886.*

Parallel to the coast is a vast park, the Sea Gardens, which were built at the beginning of the twentieth century. There you will find an aquarium, a dolphin park, a planetarium, several museums, a small zoo, and a children's park. The lovely green park features many different kinds of plants and flowers and lots of interesting statues.

▲ *Varna beach*

Burgas – the festival city

The second largest city on the Black Sea, and the fourth largest in Bulgaria, is Burgas. Burgas has a population of 195,000. It is located on the most western point of the Bay of Burgas. It sits on a peninsula surrounded by three natural lakes, swamps, and protected nature reserves (wetlands). You can see many rare birds here. Burgas is a very nice city to stay in. The atmosphere is relaxed and the climate is pleasant. There is a nice park on the top of a hill where you can look out over the sea. You can reach the beach by walking down a spiral staircase. The beach sand is unusually dark. Each year, at the end of August, the famous International Folklore Festival takes place in the Park on the Sea. In 2007, the festival celebrated its thirty-fifth anniversary. There are a number of things one can do in Burgas, which is popular with tourists because it is surrounded by breathtaking countryside. There are also many hotels, restaurants and cafés. Burgas has a smaller port than the one in Varna, but more cargo passes through its docks. Nearly three quarters of Bulgaria's imports and exports go through Burgas. The harbor attracts a lot of industry, the most important source of income for the city.

▲ *The Danube*

Ruse

Ruse lies in the north of Bulgaria on the right bank of the Danube. It has 160,000 inhabitants and is the country's fifth largest city. Romania is just across the river. Ruse is an important inland port. From Ruse you can take a ferry to the Romanian town of Giurgiu and the Ukrainian port of Reni. Ruse is the cultural and economic heart of the north. The architecture of this town on the Danube appears to be very European. It almost looks a little like Paris or Vienna.

About 200 buildings in Ruse belong to the architectural or historical heritage of Bulgaria. Dochodno Zdanie ("the profitable building") is the most famous. This old theater, dating from 1902, has a winged Mercury (the god of commerce) on the roof. Together with the Liberty Monument of 1908, it is the symbol of the city.

▶ *A pedestrian area in Ruse*

Transportation

Bulgaria is an important transit country. Major international railroads that connect Europe with Turkey and the Middle East cross the country.

▲ *Will this car still start?*

Bulgaria has an extensive and dense network of roads, totaling 25,000 miles. Because there are only 250 miles of freeways, traffic jams often occur and trips can take a long time. There are many small local roads. About 90 percent of the roads are paved.

Roads

The quality of the roads in Bulgaria is often poor. While you can certainly drive with your car on these roads, they are nowhere near as good as the roads in Western Europe. There are potholes and cracks to avoid. The bad lighting on the roads makes driving at night especially dangerous. You also have to look out for dogs on the loose. Herds of cattle that are allowed to wander might even step right out onto the road! There are a lot of horses and carts, not only on the small roads, but on the major ones as well. It is widely understood that drivers have to be alert and aware of all that is happening on Bulgarian roads.

Heavy snowfall

Sometimes, even in October, snow can become a problem. The roads outside of the cities are not in good shape, so when it snows, it's nearly impossible to drive on them. Small mountain villages outside ski resorts are often cut off from the outside world. Because many Bulgarians drive old cars, driving in the winter can sometimes be dangerous.

◀ *A driving mishap!*

▼ *Transporting goods*

Improving infrastructure

Large amounts of money are needed to repair the roads. The European Union contributes money to Bulgaria to fix its roads and improvements have been made. Through 2016, the Bulgarian government has promised to spend more than 15 billion dollars to improve the country's road infrastructure, with the building of freeways having top priority.

▶ *Enjoying a break along the railways*

More projects have to be carried out to get Bulgaria up to "European standards." Train connections within the country and with neighboring countries must be improved. A second bridge needs to be built across the Danube to Romania, and airports need to be improved and extended. Sofia expanded its airport in 2006. Most building projects have just started. Many others are behind schedule, mainly due to lack of money.

◀ *Tram and trolleybus*

Public Transportation

Public transportation is affordable. The connections are reasonable and, generally, services run on time. The problem is that, just as with the roads, too many buses, trams and, in particular, trains, are very old and need to be replaced. Most people travel by bus. About 90 percent of the populated area can be reached by bus. Only elevated and remote villages are not on a route. The bus is the most popular means of transportation because it is fast and reliable. Not all bus companies give the same quality service, however. One day you could be sitting in a bus that is thirty years old with dirty upholstery and the next day you could be in a very clean bus.

▲ *This sign reads: Children have no brakes!*

The people of Sofia, especially, use the bus often. About 85 percent of them ride the bus to work. Many children also take the bus to school, that is, if they don't walk. People have the option to ride the trolley-bus, too. Sofia's subway has been in use for more than ten years. It is, however, only 6.25 miles long. In the future, Bulgaria intends to build a subway that is more than 31 miles long with many stations.

Horse and cart in Sofia

Dimităr and his father Kamen are very poor. They must work hard every day just to eat. Thank goodness their horse does not complain very much! Their horse has been with them a long time and is pulling a cart that has an old Volkswagen Beetle on it. They are on their way to the junkyard, where this car will be completely stripped. Dimităr and Kamen will then sell the steel.

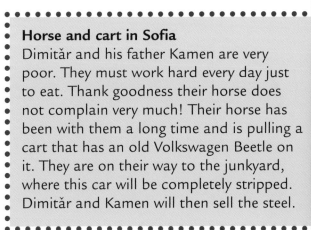

▶ *The harbor of Varna*

Shipping

Bulgaria has five important ports. The seaports Varna and Burgas on the Black Sea are important for storage. They store goods that are being shipped between Europe and the Middle East. There are three inland ports along the Danube. The one at Ruse is the biggest. It handles two-thirds of all the inland shipping. The other harbors are near Lom and Vidin. Inland shipping is decreasing and the roads are overflowing, so the European Union is providing funding to improve the navigability of the Danube and to expand and modernize the inland ports.

A second bridge over the Danube

In May 2007, a plan was approved to start building a second bridge along the 300-mile Danube border. It will lie between Calafat in Romania and Vidin in Bulgaria. Currently, you can only take the ferry. The bridge will be an important link between the Balkan countries and Central and Western Europe. The European Union and several European banks are helping to pay for this bridge. It will be nearly 1.25 miles long with four lanes and a railway line. If everything goes according to plan, it will be finished in 2011. However, there are fears that this bridge will not be completed. Lack of money, corruption, and bad organization all make such a large building project in Bulgaria frustrating.

There is only one bridge over the Danube between Bulgaria and Romania: the Friendship Bridge. It lies between Ruse and Giurgiu in Romania. It is nearly two miles long and was built in 1954.

Ferries

You can take a ferry from Varna and cross the Black Sea to two cities in the Ukraine and one in Georgia. There are a number of places where you can take a ferry across the Danube to Romania, too. A trip from Vidin to Calafat takes about 20 minutes. The ferry only leaves when it is full, which means that you might have a long wait.

Aviation

The national airline, Bulgaria Air, was set up in 2002, after the previous airline, Balkan Bulgarian Airlines, closed. The fleet consists of eleven airplanes, all of which are Boeing 737s. The three international airports are near Sofia, Varna, and Burgas. Vraždebna, near Sofia, accounts for almost 37 percent of all passenger travel. When this airport was expanded in 2006, a second runway and a second terminal were added. It had become too small and rather old-fashioned. The airports of Varna and Burgas also need some expansion. The airports in Plovdiv and Gerna Orjachovica are used mainly for freight, with limited passenger traffic.

◀ *Vraždebna airport in Sofia meets all the demands of modern air travel.*

Culture

Bulgaria has more than 7.2 million inhabitants. Of these, 84 percent are of Bulgarian descent.

◀ *A school outing in the town of Levski*

Turks are the largest minority group (about 9.5 percent). The Roma are the second largest group. The Roma are estimated to number from 350,000 to 800,000. The rest of the minority population is made up of Russians (15,000), Armenians, Vlachs, Macedonians, Greeks, and much smaller numbers of Ukrainians, Romanians, and Jews.

Unfortunately, residents of Bulgaria who are not of Bulgarian descent have historically not been treated well by the majority population. The large Turkish minority has experienced prejudice and discrimination for decades. In the 1950s, for example, Bulgaria deported about 150,000 Turkish citizens to Turkey. Turks who remained in the country were viewed by many Bulgarians as inferior citizens, people who really did not fit into Bulgarian society. Perhaps this widely held belief will begin to change with Bulgaria's admission to the European Union.

Roma

In addition to the Turks, the Roma have suffered widespread discrimination in Bulgaria over the years. Living conditions of the Roma are very poor, with many forced to live crowded together in slums. The slums breed crime and are dangerous. Trash is often left uncollected and frequently there is no electricity. Water and sewer facilities are often primitive as well, causing unsanitary conditions. This contributes to an unhealthy existence for the Roma, many of whom have little access to medical care. The Roma suffer as well economically. They are poor and large numbers are unemployed.

Estimates put the number of Roma without jobs as high as 90 percent. Addressing the plight of the Roma is a major challenge for the Bulgarian government, as well as fellow member countries of the European Union.

◀▲ *Roma play music on the train to Bansko. Having played a tune, they pass their hat around to collect money and then move on to the next train car.*

Many Roma can't read well, if they can read at all. This is because they either didn't go to school or left early. School dropout rates often predict crime rates, and this has led many Bulgarians to blame the Roma for much of the criminal behavior in the country.

More people die than babies are born. Life expectancy is quite low. On average, men only reach the age of 69 and women 77. One of the reasons for this may be the fact that Bulgarians smoke a lot. The low birth rate (about 1.4 children per woman) is leading to a decline in population as well. The infant mortality rate is very high, more than three times that in neighboring Greece. This is caused by poor health care, bad eating habits, poverty, and a low standard of living.

Decreasing population

Since 1990, the Bulgarian population has been decreasing by one percent each year.

Bulgaria

Bulgaria has the lowest population growth in the European Union. If this trend were to continue, by 2050 the population will have shrunk by as much as 35 percent. To fight this, the government is urging families to have more children. So far, this has been unsuccessful.

◄ *Two generations. If the current trend continues, there will be more elderly than young people in Bulgaria.*

Another reason why the population is shrinking is that many people are moving abroad. Between 1989 and 1995, around 800,000 Bulgarians left the country. Mostly they went to other parts of Europe or the U. S. Many Bulgarians still emigrate (especially young people) because they are dissatisfied with their economic situation, although fewer young Bulgarians are leaving now than in the 1990s.

▼ *Religion is important to many Bulgarians. Sofia is home to this ornate church.*

Religion

Most religious Bulgarians belong to the Bulgarian-Orthodox Church (83 percent). Muslims account for another 13 percent of the population, most of whom are Turks or the Pomak (Bulgarians who have converted to Islam). There are also small groups of Roman Catholics, Protestants, and Jews. During the communist era, practicing one's religion was not prohibited, but was strongly discouraged. Religious instruction was forbidden and most people didn't mention what they believed. Since the fall of communism in 1989, Bulgarians have been allowed to be openly religious again and may attend houses of worship. Freedom of religion is now part of the constitution. For more than 20 years, religious observance has increased. Many books about religion have been published and widely distributed. Bulgaria fortunately has not had the violent conflicts between members of different religious groups that other parts of the Balkans have seen.

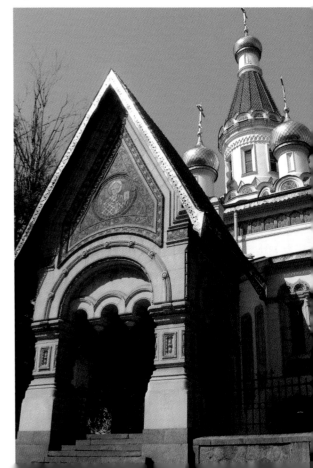

Feast days and traditions

The Orthodox-Christian religion is seen as the "traditional" or national religion. The associated feast days are very much celebrated, especially Christmas and Easter. Churches are filled at these times of year, even though not all Bulgarian Christians go to church regularly. Painting Easter eggs is an old Christian custom. One Christmas tradition is called *koleduvane*, where young men go from house to house and sing Christmas songs. On New Year's Day, Bulgarians have a feast and give each other presents. Children go from door to door wishing friends and family a Happy New Year. They carry a tree branch decorated with fruits, streamers, and treats (*survachka*). Children tap people on the shoulder with these in return for candy and money.

▲ *The annual procession in Bansko. The men are playing traditional instruments, such as the gajda (a kind of bagpipe) and the kaval (a shepherd's pipe).*

National holidays are March 3, Liberation Day (liberation from the Ottomans), and May 24. On this day the Bulgarians celebrate Bulgarian culture and the Cyrillic alphabet.

Baba Marta and martenici

A unique tradition is the celebration of Baba Marta ("Grandma March") on March 1. It announces the change from winter to summer. Baba Marta has been celebrated since the creation of the First Bulgarian Empire in 681. On this day people give each other a *martenica*. *Martenici* (plural) are red and white tassels of cotton or wool thread. They symbolize health, prosperity, and happiness. Sometimes they are attached to small dolls or cherries, but they still mean the same thing. People usually wear them as a bracelet or pin them to their shirts. According to tradition, people wear them until they see the first stork or the first flowering tree, both of which are symbols of spring. As soon as you see either, you hang your *martenica* on the branch of a fruit tree. That symbolizes fertility. You can also hide it under a rock, which drives out the evil spirits from man and nature.

Wedding in Vraca

Rosica and Nadežda are cousins. Today they are bridesmaids because their aunt Maria is getting married. Maria has been nervous the whole day and is constantly adjusting the girls' dresses. Rosica and Nadežda don't like that very much. They also have to wait for hours and the dresses are uncomfortable.

I wish it was finished .... This dress is itchy!

Customs, habits, and free time

Bulgarians love to visit each other. When they enter a house, they take off their shoes. They always bring a little present with them, too. Guests are made to feel right at home. The table is full of food and as soon as your plate goes empty, it is filled up again. Refusing more food is considered bad manners.

Bulgarian boys

Anton, brothers Todor and Živko, Vasil, Petko, and Dimitar are good friends. It's summer vacation now and they can do all sorts of things together from early in the morning to late at night. They only go home for their lunch and dinner. They play in the woods, build huts, and play by the river that runs through their village. They may even take some fruit from the orchard that belongs to Mr. Atanas. He will, of course, chase them with a stick in his hand, yelling at them.

Well...come on! Let's go play!

Bulgarian children love computer games and more and more use the Internet. Online chat programs are popular. The Internet is not available everywhere and connections are often slow. It is also very expensive.

▶ *Brother and sister*

▶ A Bulgarian ambulance. The word "ambulance" is written backwards on the hood so that you can read it in your rearview mirror.

Medical care

During the communist era, people could visit the doctor and the hospital free of charge, although care and medical equipment were not exactly of the best quality. Since 1998, medical care has not been provided by the government. People who work must pay for medical insurance. Unemployed people have difficulty getting medical insurance. In reality, about 1 million people are uninsured. Many of these are the Roma.

◀ Changing the guard at the presidential palace in Sofia

Government and parliament

Bulgaria has 28 *oblasts*, which are provinces or districts. They have the same name as the main towns. Plovdiv is the capital of oblast Plovdiv. The capital Sofia is an oblast by itself. Every oblast is divided into municipalities.

The country is a parliamentary republic with a "one chamber parliament," known as the *Narodno Săbranie*, or "national assembly." There is no Upper Chamber, only a Lower Chamber of Parliament. It consists of 240 members who are elected for a period of four years. The Bulgarian president is elected directly by the people for a period of five years.

Hospitals often work with old equipment and there are not enough ambulances. The people are dissatisfied with the changes made since 1998. A lot of people complain that their life has actually become worse and less healthy now that it is more difficult to afford medical care. A visit to the doctor is still affordable, but not an operation or a visit to the dentist. For that, you have to pay extra. Nearly all Bulgarians who can afford to do these things take out private medical insurance. The government has promised to privatize the medical sector (make it independent of government control), but it hasn't reached that point yet.

▼ The Bulgarian Parliament Building

◄ *Businessmen display their fresh produce at an open market, a common sight in Bulgaria.*

Corruption

A persistent problem throughout Bulgarian society is widespread corruption. This exists within all layers of the population. Bulgarians think it is quite normal to bribe a doctor in a hospital so that they can be helped more quickly, or pay off a policeman who has given them a ticket because their taillight is not working. Corruption, bribery, and favoritism are normal at the highest levels of society. In government and the civil service, it is more expected than surprising. A lot of people, from ministries to municipalities, have obtained their jobs through political contacts. They were not given the job because they delivered good work or deserved the position. When Bulgaria became a member of the European Union in 2007, officials at EU headquarters in Brussels, Belgium were very worried. Something had to be done. But for the Bulgarians, corruption is not unusual. Illegal practices and ignoring wrongdoing, together with bribery and avoiding taxes, are widely accepted actions.

Language and the Cyrillic alphabet

Bulgarian is a South Slavic language, just like Serbo-Croatian, Bosnian, Macedonian, and Slovene. Apart from the inhabitants of Bulgaria, there are various minorities in Greece, Romania, and Moldova that speak the Bulgarian language. Like the Serbs and Russians, the Bulgarians use the Cyrillic alphabet. This is derived from the alphabet that the monks Methodius and Cyrillus developed on the orders of the Byzantine emperor in the ninth century. Later on, upon the request of King Boris, students of these two monks developed an alphabet that looked like Greek but with a number of letters that produced typical Slavic sounds.

▶ *This is what Bulgarian-Cyrillic script looks like. This poster with a cartoon of the Bulgarian actress Tanja Masalitinova can be seen in Theater 199's Hall of Fame in Sofia. The artist is Ivajlo Ninov.*

Bulgarian	Pronunciation	Translation
Да	Dah	*Yes*
Не	Nee	*No*
Моля	Molya	*Please (request)*
Заповядайте	Zadovolyavam	*Please (giving)*
Благодаря	Blagodarya	*Thanks*
Довиждане	Dovizhdanee	*Goodbye*
Извинете	Izvinete	*Excuse me*
Как си/сте?	Kak ste see	*How are you?*
Здравейте	Zdraveyte	*Hello*
Съжалявам!	Soozhalyavam	*Sorry!*
Наздраве!	Nazdrave	*To your health!*
Добро утро	Dobro utro	*Good morning*
Не разбирам	Nee razbiram	*I (don't) understand*
Обичам те	Obicham te	*I love you*
Къде е тоалетната?	Koode e toaletnata	*Where is the toilet?*

▲ *Traditional dance*

Čalga music

Čalga music is extremely popular all over the Balkans. The Serbian variety is known as *turbo folk*, the Greek type is called *Laïká,* and the Romanian is *Mani*. Čalga is a mixture of local folk music with Turkish and Arabian musical influences and slower gypsy melodies. A hard, pumping beat pervades this music. Čalga singers, often young girls performing attractive dance steps, sing about love and betrayal. People in bars sometimes sing along to these songs. Many Bulgarians think Čalga is the result of a lack of culture. They think the music seems to be that of the uneducated youth and vulgar people. But if that is true, then nobody in Bulgaria can be called educated because Čalga is more popular than any other kind of music!

Dance and music

Many Bulgarians think that during the five centuries of Ottoman occupation there was no room to develop their own culture. This, however, is not true. Old traditions and customs were passed on from one generation to the next, especially in more remote areas of the country. Stories, legends, and typical Bulgarian folk music have survived throughout the passage of time. Typical for this type of folk music are the intricate asymmetric rhythms and melodies, and the way in which the singers use their voices. They press the larynx, where the vocal chords are located, to produce a particular vibrating sound. A well-known Bulgarian folk dance is the *choro*, a whirling circle dance. There are all kinds of variations. It is danced in other Eastern European countries as well.

▼ *Dancing and having fun at a New Year's party*

Traditional Bulgarian instruments often look like Turkish ones. They are found all over the Balkans, just like the music that is played with them. The most important, widely used instrument is the *gajda*, a kind of bagpipe made from goat or sheep skin, which produces one low, long, drawn-out note. Other instruments include the *gadulka*, violin-like, but played vertically on the knee with a bow, and the *kaval*, a long shepherd's pipe that makes a muffled, sad sound.

Education

Since the revolution in 1989, public education has decreased in quality. Government funding for schools is at levels far below that of most EU countries.

While the government pays for school in the elementary and secondary grades, both pre-school and college expenses must be paid by the families of students.

▲ *Playing outside in Plovdiv Park. These pre-school children have a lot of time for play. Public school education doesn't start until age seven.*

In most EU countries, the government pays tuition for students up through the university. In Bulgaria, families are expected to pay for nursery school, kindergarten, and post-secondary school education. Books and "extras," such as activities outside of school, are also the families' responsibility, as are the costs of exams that students must take to advance to each level of education.

Reading and writing

Almost everyone in Bulgaria can read and write. Only one percent of the population is illiterate (people who cannot read or write). Unfortunately, this does not include the Roma, whose illiteracy rate is about 18.5 percent. Not even half of the Roma finish primary school. Only nine percent graduate from secondary school. Fifteen years ago, though, less than five percent graduated. While this represents an improvement, higher education is nearly impossible for the Roma.

Compulsory education

All Bulgarian children must go to school between the ages of seven and sixteen. Even before they are seven, many children attend nursery school or kindergarten. Nearly everyone completes primary school. Most children, about 90 percent, then go to secondary school. Three-quarters of them graduate.

Where is the bus?

School outing in Levski

These preschool children are standing at the bus station in the town of Levski. They are waiting for the bus to take them back to their village. They are four to five years old. Today they have been on a school outing. First they went to the theater and then for a Happy Meal at McDonald's. They are tired from their exciting day. Now it's time to go home.

Grades on children's work varies from 2 to 6. A very bad grade is "2" and an excellent grade is "6." A "3" is similar to a "D" in the United States.

Primary education

Bulgarians think that education is very important. The "classical" method of teaching was encouraged during the communist era. This involved memorizing material, being tested on it, and doing homework. This teaching method is still typical, even in primary school. Knowing many facts is typically emphasized more than independent thinking or group studies. Subjects such as handicrafts, drawing, and music are seldom taught. Children who have trouble memorizing facts in many subjects at once often have difficulty keeping up. Learning how to write essays is also important for Bulgarian students, as is the study of foreign languages. Childen are taught English in primary school. Before 1989, all children were forced to learn Russian. Once students enter secondary school, a second foreign language is added to their class schedules.

▲ *School children hanging around in the old town center of Plovdiv*

The introduction of dancing and handicraft classes helps to develop an individual's talents and interests. Education and training in these subjects is limited, but still receives some attention.

A school day

On average, children go to school for five hours a day. That is less than in the United States. Instead, Bulgarian children must spend a lot of time doing their homework, about three hours every day. The school day is divided into mornings and afternoons. The school year is divided into two terms: mid-September to January and January to June. During one term, you can go to school in the morning, and during the other term in the afternoon. Children at primary school can do their homework at school during the "free" part of the school day. A teacher is always there to help. If children don't stay at school, they do their homework at home. Whole families live together in one house, including grandparents. Most of the time there is someone at home to take care of the children before they go to school and when they come home. Very often it is a grandmother.

The start of the school year is a festive occasion. Many parents bring their children to school on the first day and the teacher welcomes everybody. Some children give their teachers bunches of flowers.

These grades will get us a reward!

Report cards

Aleksandăr and his sister Ivanka are excited. The last day of school before summer vacation has just finished. They both have received good grades on their report cards. Ivanka is very proud of hers. "I am sure that Mom and Dad will like this report card!"

◀ *Classmates ready to begin their school day. Let's hope the teacher will show up soon so class can get started!*

Secondary education

At the end of year six or seven (depending on the type of secondary education) pupils have to choose a secondary school: a technical school (training in a specific vocation) or a grammar school, where general knowledge and languages are emphasized.

Some secondary schools pay a lot of attention to teaching foreign languages. To be admitted to this kind of school, you first have to pass the compulsory exam in year seven. All secondary schools teach the same compulsory subjects, such as math, literature, foreign languages, history, and biology. You can also take optional subjects such as dancing, Turkish, or general religious instruction. The schools can choose what kind of textbooks they want to use. Under communism, the government decided which books to use.

Vocational training

Since 1989, vocational training has been severely affected by the cutbacks in funds for education. Many teachers have been dismissed. The teaching material is out of date and does not match up to today's standards. There is very little money available for teaching equipment and good computers. The computers that are available are often old and slow. Teachers' salaries are low and there is very little enthusiasm to become a teacher. Some teachers have gone to teach in private schools or have gone into business. In general, the standard of teaching has declined.

Higher education

In higher education, some studies cost more than others. Private schools have fees that can sometimes rise dramatically. Higher education has become impossibly expensive for Bulgarians. The tuition fees to study medicine at the university are almost three thousand dollars. This is in a country where the average salary is around 250 dollars per month. Many students do not complete their studies. These days, fewer young people go to the university than did under communism. Some of the brightest young people seek their fortune abroad. They travel to universities that allow them to study on a scholarship. Though now quite costly to attend, Bulgaria has more than 40 institutes of higher learning, which includes four "old" universities. The most important and the oldest is in Sofia. It was founded in 1888. The other universities are in Plovdiv, Veliko Tărnovo, and Blagoevgrad.

Private education

The first private school was established in 1991, though few Bulgarian children go to private schools. The number is growing, however, because many families believe they do a better job of educating children than the state schools do.

▶ *The Paisii Hilendarski University in Plovdiv*

Cuisine

Bulgarian food is "Balkan food." It was influenced by many different countries. It is a little bit Slav, a little bit Middle Eastern, and mostly Greek, Serbian, and Turkish.

Most hotels, especially in the tourist areas, serve "international food." This means that the dishes are not typically Bulgarian. If you want to eat Bulgarian food, you go to a *mechana*, or a folk restaurant. The menu contains authentic Bulgarian dishes. Folk music is often played during the meal, too! The waiters are dressed in national dress and, if people are in the mood, they will break into folk dances.

▲ *In a mechana*

Vegetables

Many vegetables are used in Bulgarian cooking. Due to the good climate and greenhouses, vegetables are on the menu throughout the whole year. Main dish and side salads are served everywhere. Bulgarians also love vegetables that are preserved in oil or are pickled.

Vegetarian food

Vegetarians still have difficulties getting "meat-free" main courses. Although the Bulgarians like eating salads and vegetables, those are rarely the main dish of a meal. For vegetarians, it just takes a little mixing and matching

to find a dish that is suitable. You can choose from the different kinds of salads. The ingredients for a typical Bulgarian salad are cabbage, tomatoes, cucumbers, red peppers, and onions. Bulgarians especially love onions. Salads are eaten from one big bowl and everyone can use their own fork to pick and choose what they want.

▶ *It is not easy to find a meat-free main course. Most Bulgarians love to eat meat.*

There are also many dishes made with cheese. *Sirene* is a typical Bulgarian cheese. It is white and salty and very tasty. It tastes like feta cheese. Vegetarians can also choose one of the several thick vegetable soups. *Bob čorba* (bean soup) is the most well known and can be bought everywhere.

▲ *Meze*

Bulgarian yogurt (*kiselo mljako*)
Bulgarian yogurt is world famous. This dairy product contains a unique microorganism called *Lactobacillus bulgaricus,* which gives the yogurt a distinctive taste. It is thicker and fuller than the yogurt we know. First, the milk from which it is made is thickened. *Kiselo mljako* has been around for a long time. Even the ancient Thracians ate it!

Tarator is also quite tasty. It is a cold soup, though some think it is more like a liquid salad. It is based on yogurt, cucumber, garlic, and dill. It also contains oil, water, and walnuts. In the summer especially, it is a popular side dish. It is also eaten as an appetizer.

Meze and rakija

Meze are small snacks that are served with alcoholic drinks, like *rakija*. Rakija is a brandy made from distilled, fermented fruit. It is served all over the Balkans. However, the fruits from which the drink is distilled vary from region to region. The Serbs use plums and the rakija is known as *slivovič.* In Bulgaria, they use grapes. Rakija distilled from grapes is called *grozdova* or *grozdovica.* If the drink is made from Muscat grapes, it is called *muskatova.* Some may think that the Bulgarians drink a lot, but the more careful drinkers make sure to eat meze as they drink. Salads are usually eaten with meze, along with different kinds of cheese and vegetables preserved in oil. Sausage is very popular, too. *Lukanka* is a spicy salami with a strong flavor. There is also *sudžuk,* which is the Bulgarian version of the Turkish *sucuk.* It is made from beef and varies in taste from strong to very strong. Bulgarians also eat bread with just about everything.

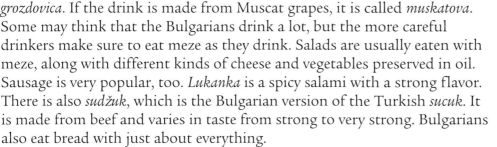

◀ *Rakija distillery*

▲ *A glass of rakija and a glass of ajrjan (non-alcoholic yogurt drink)*

In Bulgaria it is quite common to sit at the table for about an hour and a half to enjoy a couple of glasses of alcohol with meze. Then the proper meal starts. The Bulgarians generally drink wine with their main course. Water or beer are other options. Bulgarian wine, especially red wine, has an excellent reputation all over the world. The wines are strong. The strongest are usually from the grapes used in the Cabernet Sauvignon or the Merlot wines.

◀ Roast lamb is a favorite. It is usually served on Saint George's Day on May 6.

Meat dishes

Bulgarians like to eat their meat grilled. Lamb is the most popular, then pork. Sometimes wild boar shows up on the menu. Popular grilled meat dishes are *kebapčeta* and *kjufteta*. Kebapčeta are little rolls. Kjufteta are small round balls of strongly seasoned minced meat. *Kavărma* is an everyday stew with vegetables and meat, usually pork. It is eaten frequently in Bulgarian homes.

▼ A kiosk selling nuts and dried fruit

Kavărma looks like Hungarian goulash. The evening meal often starts with soup or salad, or both. Then it is followed by either grilled meat or a stew with potatoes for the main course. For dessert there is baklava, a very sweet dish made from layers of puff pastry with honey and walnuts.

Bulgarian breakfast: banica and boza

Bulgarians love pies made from puff pastry. You can buy all sorts of pastries (some sweet, some slightly salty). These pastries are found at small stalls on nearly every street corner. When freshly baked, the pastries are very delicious. According to the Bulgarians, the pastry called *banica* is the very essence of Bulgarian food. Banica is baked in an oven. It is made from beaten eggs and sirene cheese. This is put between layers of puff pastry. It can be varied sometimes with either a spinach or a sweet filling. The cheese-filled kind is the most common. Bulgarians don't take much time to eat breakfast. They usually just grab a piece of *banica* and drink a glass of *kiselo mljako* or *ajrjan* (a salty liquid yogurt drink). However, usually they grab *boza*. Boza is a thick, brown colored liquid with a slightly sour taste. It tastes a little like cornflakes with milk.

Šopska salad (serves 4)

Ingredients:
- 5-7 ounces green onions (or 1 big onion)
- 4 medium-sized tomatoes
- 5-7 ounces feta cheese, grated
- 1 green pepper and 1 red pepper
- 1 small cucumber
- 1 small pimento pepper
- 2 tablespoons oil and 1 tablespoon vinegar

Peel and dice the onion. Wash the tomatoes and cut them into small slices. Mix onion and tomatoes together. Peel the cucumber and cut it into pieces. Wash the peppers, remove the seeds, and cut them into small pieces. Add the peppers and cucumbers to the tomatoes and onion. Pour oil and vinegar over the mixture and add salt and pepper to taste. Sprinkle cheese and thinly sliced pimento pepper rings over the top.

◀ This salad features olives instead of pimento peppers.

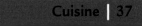

Economy

January 1, 2007 was a historic day for Bulgaria. Together with its neighbor Romania, the country joined the European Union.

This was a historic day because Bulgaria has always seen itself as a European country, despite the Turkish occupation. With the entrance into the EU, the country's European status was confirmed. The EU could now help Bulgaria recover from its deep economic crisis.

▲ *Work is still done using old equipment and materials. Here though, the horse and cart have been replaced.*

Bulgaria is slowly building a good and stable economy through large reforms. However, the income and living standards of Bulgarians are still far below that of other Europeans.

The economy under communism

Before World War II, Bulgaria was mainly an agricultural country. That changed when the communists gained power in 1944. They quickly turned Bulgaria into an industrialized country. Agriculture was nationalized, meaning that the land was taken under the government's control. Individual farmers and their families had to give up their land. From then on, the government decided what and how much food to grow. Agriculture was turned into a collective, large-scale business.

▼ *Women as well as men work the land.*

▶ *Advertising is part of a free economy. There is always instant coffee for those who do not like strong Turkish coffee.*

It is typical of a communist-led economy that the government decides supply and demand, not the consumers, or the citizens. This meant Bulgarians had few choices about what goods to buy. The only items produced were the ones that the government thought the people needed. For the most part, the country traded with other communist countries for goods produced whether people really wanted them or not.

Moving towards a free-market economy

This all changed with the fall of communism in 1989. Trade, including exports to Bulgaria's communist neighbors, fell off dramatically. Personal income declined considerably. Government pensions, or money people receive when they retire, were no longer paid. Many people were unemployed. There was not enough food and not enough energy. For many, the years after communist rule ended were extremely difficult.

▲ *The older generation found it hard to have hope in these dark times.*

Bulgaria needed to become a free-market economy. This is an economy in which buyers and sellers in the market determine the prices of goods and services. The process of change in Bulgaria's economy took a long time because government officials were slow to make reforms. Many were too busy making themselves rich off of formerly state-owned property, such as manufacturing plants. As a result, in 1996–1997 Bulgaria landed in a deep economic crisis, including strikes and political demonstrations. A new, non-communist government was finally able to improve the situation.

From 1997 onward, significant reforms took place. Bulgaria's lev was supported by the German mark and then later by the euro, Europe's common currency. The government privatized state enterprises. This means that factories and companies, as well as farms, were once again privately owned. People were suffering but, in time, the economy began to improve.

▶ *Almost no country in the world is without a McDonald's.*

I wish spring would come ....

The present Bulgarian economy

Since 1996-1997, the economy has improved. The yearly growth rate of the economy is five percent. Unemployment has decreased considerably. Wages, however, are still lower than in the rest of the EU. The cost of living is lower as well, but not by much. The government has not yet succeeded in stopping corruption in the court system or civil service (such as the police or customs officials). As a member of the EU, Bulgaria receives subsidies (money) to raise the country up to higher European living standards. Bulgaria has been warned by the EU that if corruption is not eliminated quickly, support from the EU will drop.

The "gray economy"

The informal, or gray, economy is a big problem. This means that people don't pay taxes on the money they earn from their work. Because of this, the government goes without millions of dollars a year. The gray economy is so widespread because most Bulgarians can barely live on their small wages alone. Many look for ways to make a little extra money. Some have small plots of land given to them so they can grow their own food, while others distill their own liquor, such as rakija. Many people have jobs, but also earn money through the gray economy. They will make household repairs and do odd jobs around town. They also drive taxis, look after young children, or care for the elderly.

▲ *This store in Pleven sells tools and materials used in building and improving homes.*

Industry

Bulgaria's most important industries are electricity, gas, water, chemicals, iron and steel, engineering and construction, food, alcoholic beverages, and tobacco. The information technologies market is also growing rapidly, with sales of computer hardware for home use in particular expanding.

◄ *Garden-grown tomatoes for sale! Many people add to their incomes by selling produce from home.*

▶ *The Studen Kladenec Dam on the Arda River in the Rodopi Mountains helps to generate electricity.*

Foreign companies are investing in the country to get more Bulgarians to use computers, credit cards, and mobile phones. The EU is also investing money to expand sales of consumer goods.

Import and export

Bulgaria exports many items. Among them are clothing, shoes, iron, and steel, machinery and parts, fuel and chemicals. Vegetables, such as tomatoes and peppers, and fruit, such as apples and grapes, are also exported. The country is also known for its tobacco, brandy, wine, sunflowers, rose oil, and the famous Bulgarian yogurt (see page 36). In recent years, fruit exports have declined, while wine sales have increased. Bulgaria's main export partners are Italy, Germany, Turkey, and Greece. Belgium and France are also starting to receive more of Bulgaria's exports.

Oil, gas, and iron ore are imported. Plastics, chemicals, machinery and parts are also imported. Russia provides fuel, though it hardly buys anything from Bulgaria. For the last couple of years, Bulgarians have spent more on goods from Russia than from any other country. This is because prices for oil have risen. About 17 percent of Bulgaria's imports come from Russia. Other import partners are Germany, Italy, Turkey, and now, increasingly, China.

▲ *A tobacco plant drying shed in the Rodopi Mountains. Tobacco is a product Bulgaria exports.*

Rose oil

The Valley of Roses is located near the town of Kazanlăk, between the Balkan Mountains and the Sredna Gora Mountains. The Bulgarian *Rosa Damascena* grows here. It is also known as the Damascus Rose. The plant has been cultivated here for more than 300 years because of the world-famous rose oil it produces. During May the valley turns a beautiful red and the air is filled with the sweet scent of roses. The petals are harvested in June. A complex process is used to extract the oil from the petals. You need 6,600 pounds of rose petals to produce one liter (33.8 fluid ounces) of rose oil. Not surprising, pure rose oil is very expensive. It is used in perfumes, creams, and soaps, and can also be found in alcoholic drinks, jam, and chocolate. Rose oil is even used to flavor pills! The Rose Festival takes place in Kazanlăk at the beginning of June, right around harvest time.

▲ *The beach at Varna*

Tourism

In the communist era, the Black Sea was a popular place for many people from Bulgaria and the rest of the Eastern bloc to spend their vacations.

Only recently have tourists from countries beyond the former communist East come to spend their vacations in Bulgaria. Modern hotels and resorts will attract even more.

Foreign tourists come primarily to visit the Black Sea coast. Many of the vacationers also ski, hike, and admire the cultural heritage in places such as Plovdiv and Sofia.

▶ *The palace in Evksinograd*

The beach and the Black Sea

Nearly three-quarters of all tourists come to Bulgaria to enjoy the sun, sea, and beach. The Bulgarians themselves like to spend their vacations along the Black Sea coast. The beach is 100 miles long. The two beach resorts are in Varna in the north and Burgas in the south. Both towns have enormous tourist areas, such as Sunny Beach and Golden Sands, where prices for lodging are not too high. While the beach resorts offer tourists a place to relax, visitors can also step into Bulgaria's colorful past. For a taste of historic

Bulgaria, one can visit Evksinograd, a former royal summer palace near Varna. Another historic place along the coast is Nesebăr, a small medieval town just north of Burgas.

Winter sports

Bulgarians have always known that their country is ideal for winter sports. In recent years, foreigners have discovered the country's winter appeal, too. The mountains of Pirin, Rila, Rodopi, Vitoša, and the Balkans offer many opportunities to enjoy winter activities. The best time to go skiing, snowboarding, or cross-country skiing is between November and March, when extensive snow coverage can be counted on.

The largest ski resorts are in Borovec (in the Rila Mountains) and Pamporovo (in the Rodopi Mountains). Bansko is quite new, but has already been discovered by many tourists. The surroundings are absolutely beautiful. Bansko is in the Pirin National Park. There are good winter sports facilities and the little town has much to offer.

◀ *Plenty of good snow for winter sports*

◄ *The Snežanka Cave has beautiful stalactites and stalagmites.*

Hiking and mountain climbing

During the summer many people hike among these same mountains or go climbing. More than one-third of the country consists of mountains, so there are plenty of opportunities for these activites. Bulgarians are skilled hikers. Hiking in the mountains is their favorite pastime. They are very fond of the high Balkan Mountains. Not all the paths in the high mountains are well marked or passable, and it is wise to be well-equipped for them or to go with a guide. The paths in the central part of the Balkan Mountains, between the Valley of Roses and the Danube Lowlands, are passable. The Rodopi Mountains in the south are also hikers' and nature lovers' favorites. The varied scenery of rugged forests and lovely Alpine meadows are a beautiful sight. Bulgaria has three national parks: Pirin, Rila, and Central Balkan National Park. Adventurous tourists can have a lot of fun exploring hundreds of caves throughout Bulgaria.

Old villages and towns

Sofia and Plovdiv are popular attractions worth seeing. Most visitors, however, find Bulgaria is at its most beautiful in the countryside. In the magnificent mountains and in the valleys such as Rila and Pirin you'll find small villages and towns such as Bansko and Koprivštica. Here you can breathe in the atmosphere of times long past. Veliko Tărnovo, the medieval capital of the Second Bulgarian Empire, is one such small town. It is full of historical monuments, such as the ruins of Carevec castle. In the mountains you can find several other forts.

Nesebăr

Nesebăr is an old fishing village on the Black Sea. In the past it was a harbor town. The houses in the old part of the village are full of architectural, historical, and archaeological monuments from various periods. It is extraordinary how much has been preserved. In Nesebăr, layer upon layer of different civilizations lie on top of one another. The oldest archaeological layers go back more than 3,000 years. Nesebăr is on UNESCO's World Heritage List. In the summer the old town can get quite crowded, but outside of the tourist season, it is much quieter. Church ruins dating from the Byzantine, Bulgarian, and Ottoman empires attract many visitors. The oldest ruins date from the fifth century.

▲ *The Orlov bridge (Eagle Bridge) in Sofia, which was designed by the Proseks, a Czech family of architects*

▼ *Historic ruins in Nesebăr*

In the Monastery of Rila
These women clean the monastery. Though they work in the most beautiful place in Bulgaria, it is still a rough job. The floors and tiles must be polished daily. The windows must be cleaned very carefully. When it snows, the work is twice as hard. The snow brought in from the soles of thousands of visitors' shoes must be cleaned up. Now though, it is break time. Radka, the woman with the baby, is still on maternity leave. She will start working again next week.

Are you ready to come back to work?

The Monastery of Rila

There are many monasteries in Bulgaria. Some are far away in the mountains and difficult to reach. The largest monasteries are those of Trojan, Rožen, Bačkovo, and Rila. Rila is the best known and is on UNESCO's World Heritage List. The Monastery of Rila was founded in the tenth century to house monks who wanted to lead a life of prayer apart from the world. In the Middle Ages, however, it grew into a spiritual and social center for the Orthodox-Christian believers. The monastery's architecture is impressive. It's set in the Rila Mountains in a beautiful location between two small mountain rivers, the Rilska and the Drušljavica. Buses full of tourists come to visit the monastery and enjoy the silence, the surroundings, and the religious art.

The Madara Knight

The Madara Knight is a relief sculpture carved into the sheer cliffs of the Madara Plateau near Shumen in northeast Bulgaria. The relief, a little over 75 feet tall, is a horseman who has pierced a lion with his spear. The lion lies at the feet of the man's horse. A dog is running behind the horseman. The relief is thought to have been made by the Proto-Bulgarians. These people, along with the Slavs, were the original Bulgarians. Around the relief are three partially preserved texts. These texts are from three different periods of time. The earliest text is from 710. Some scholars think the sculpture was made by the Thracians and could represent a Thracian god. The relief was added to UNESCO's World Heritage list in 1979.

◀ *The Preobraženski Monastery*

Nature

Because of the country's varied climate, Bulgaria's plant and animal life is quite diverse. In the north, the climate is continental. In the south and east, toward the Black Sea, the climate is Mediterranean. The Balkan Range divides the country in two.

▲ *Snakeroot grows on Vitoša. The flower is thought to cure snakebite and heal other ailments.*

Regional differences in climate account for the rich variety found in Bulgaria's plant and animal life.

Plant and animal life

There are 3,700 different kinds of plants in Bulgaria. Of these, 250 are unique to the country. They include the Rila primrose, the Balkan violet, and the Rodopi tulip.

The mountain areas contain extensive forests. About 30 percent of the country is forested. A long time ago, this figure was higher, but forests were cut down to create agricultural land and other development. You can still find thick, broad-leafed forests of oak, beech, elm, ash, and wild chestnut in the Balkan Mountains and parts of Rila, Pirin, and Rodopi.

A very rare animal lives near the coast of the Black Sea. It's called the Mediterranean Monk Seal, now considered a critically endangered species. There are only about 500 left in the entire world and sightings of the animal anywhere are very infrequent.

▲ *There are donkeys here, too.*

Higher in the mountains, the vegetation is Alpine. Conifer trees and the rare edelweiss grow here. No other EU country has as many animal species as Bulgaria. There are about 13,000 species, including fish, mammals, birds, amphibians, and insects.

▶ *On the lookout for interesting wildlife along the Black Sea coast*

Birds

Bulgaria is both home to many species of birds and located on the route of many migrating birds. The country hosts about 400 different kinds of birds, including the very large Imperial Eagle. There are only about 2,000 eagles of this kind left in the whole world, including some in Hungary and Slovakia. Another threatened species, the Red-necked Goose, also lives in Bulgaria. The goose is a winter guest. In the countryside one may see beautiful colonies of storks and swallows. The specially created wetlands, or protected nature reserves, are very important for the survival of amphibians and breeding winter guests, such as the pelican.

▶ *Kissing the frog?*

Wild animals

Wolves, bears, wild boar, and wild cats live on the lower slopes of the heavily forested mountains. There are still some jackals, but they are now very rare. The lynx has just about disappeared. Some animals, such as the wild mountain goat (chamois) and the pelican, only live in nature reserves.

The brown bear lives all over the Balkan Mountains, but its numbers are declining. There are still about 800 living freely in the wild. The bear was recently put on the list of protected animals and, with few exceptions, may no longer be hunted.

Endangered animals

Bulgaria's wildlife population has suffered from deforestation. Deforestation and land development have made many animals' natural habitat smaller and smaller. Excessive hunting and poaching have also reduced the numbers of many animals. Of the 100 mammal species living in Bulgaria, nearly half are now protected by the government.

National parks and nature reserves

Three national parks, ten nature parks, and about 90 nature reserves have been created to protect plants, flowers, and animals. Nature reserves in particular have been established to protect and restore plant and animal life, although this work is also carried out in the national parks. The protection of rare breeds about to go extinct is especially important in the nature reserves. However, enough space has been left in them for limited recreational use by the public. Nearly five percent of the total land area in the country is protected.

▲ *The Woodchat Shrike is a small bird of prey that lives in marshlands.*

Dancing bears

For years, bears were made to dance in public for the entertainment of people. Now it is no longer allowed. The last dancing bear was freed in the summer of 2007. The bears now live in the dancing bear park in Belica in southwestern Bulgaria. The park is managed by the Brigitte Bardot Foundation and the Organization for Four-footers. These groups are dedicated to defending animal rights and to helping injured animals. After a horrible life dancing, the bears can now lead a more natural existence. In their former life, dancing bears had a miserable time. They ate poor food that was often too sweet and had to learn to "dance" on hot coals. A bear's nose was pierced with a large ring that was attached to a chain. For the majority of owners, mostly Roma, keeping bears was a family tradition as well as a way to make money. In Bulgaria, the ban on dancing bears was proclaimed in 1993. The ban does not apply to Russia, Ukraine, and Serbia.

Nature conservation

Sadly, protected areas have not been managed well. The mountainous areas and those near the sea have suffered the most. They get the most traffic because tourists are interested in seeing them. Though tourism helps Bulgaria's economy, it can also hurt the cause of conserving nature. The Bansko Ski Center, built in the protected Pirin National Park, is one place where this is happening. The park is on the UNESCO World Heritage List for its special biodiversity, vast lands, and unspoiled nature. It will be a challenge there to strike the right balance between tourism and preserving nature.

Areas on the Black Sea that were protected have been opened up to project developers. Now hotels and vacation homes are being built on this land. If not managed properly, development could destroy the natural beauty of the region, something the EU will work with Bulgaria to prevent.

▶ *A land development project being completed in the Rodopi Mountains*

Environmental Issues

After 1989 it became clear how much the Bulgarian environment had suffered from heavy industry in the communist economy. Soil and air were badly polluted. Environmental protection had not been a priority for the communists. There were no measures taken to help the environment recover until the 1990s. Government-run heavy industries had polluted the environment on a large scale. They discarded, drained, and dumped pollutants, harming the ground, the water, and the air. According to estimates made in 1991, 60 percent of agricultural land and two thirds of all rivers were contaminated. The Danube and Black Sea are badly polluted from chemicals, open sewers, and heavy metals. More than a quarter of the forests are affected by air pollution and acid rain. For the past 10 years, however, caring for the environment has been a very important issue for the government and the people.

◀ *A recycling container in Stara Zagora. The sign says, "Working together for a cleaner Bulgaria."*

Glossary

Balkan Peninsula Also called the Balkans, a region of southeastern Europe formerly ruled by the Ottoman Turks including the modern countries of Bulgaria, Greece, Serbia, Macedonia, Bosnia-Herzegovina, Kosovo, Montenegro, and Albania.

Communism A political system based on the principles of government control of property and public speech.

Constitution A series of laws outlining the basic principles of a government or country.

Eastern Bloc The countries of eastern Europe that came under communist rule led by the Soviet Union after World War II, lasting until 1989.

Ottoman Empire A great Muslim power, based in Turkey, that conquered and ruled much of Europe for centuries until 1918, with its defeat in World War I.

Roma An ethnic group, also called Gypsies, that suffers from poverty and discrimination across much of Europe, particularly in the Balkans.

UNESCO United Nations Educational, Scientific, and Cultural Organization, established to promote education and communication.

Index

Websites

https://www.cia.gov/library/publications/the-world-factbook/geos/bu.html
www.bulgariatravel.org
www.lonelyplanet.com/bulgaria
http://www.worldstatesmen.org/Bulgaria.html
http://www.britannica.com/EBchecked/topic/84090/Bulgaria